FIRE ENGINES

Ann Becker

This edition first published in 2010 in the United States of America by Marshall Cavendish Benchmark.

Marshall Cavendish Benchmark
99 White Plains Road
Tarrytown, NY 10591
www.marshallcavendish.us

All Internet addresses were available and accurate when this book was sent to press.

Library of Congress Cataloging-in-Publication Data

Becker, Ann, 1965-
    Fire engines / by Ann Becker.
        p. cm. -- (Amazing machines)
        Summary: "Discusses the different kinds of fire engines, what they are used for, and how they work"--Provided by publisher.
        Includes bibliographical references and index.
        ISBN 978-0-7614-4403-9
1. Fire engines--Juvenile literature. I. Title.
    TH9372.B43 2010
    628.9'259--dc22
    2008054370

JNF
628.9
BECKER

The photographs in this book are used by permission and through the courtesy of:
t=top b=bottom c=center l=left r=right m=middle
Cover Photos: Rysick Photography/Shutterstock; Inset: Shutterstock; BG Len Tillim/iStockphoto
Half Title Photo: Robert.

P4-5: Stan Kujawa/PhotographerDirect; P6-7: Q2AMedia Image Bank; P8-9: Lucidio Studio, Inc./Jupiter images; P9(inset): Nick Ut/
Associated Press; P10-11: Q2AMedia Image Bank; P11(inset): Q2AMedia Image Bank; P12-13: Oglesby Fire Department: P13(inset):
Jim West/Alamy; P14-15: Q2AMedia Image Bank; P15(inset): Ian Marlow/PhotographerDirects; P16-17: Nero/BigStockPhoto;
P17(inset): Shutterstock; P18-19: Robert; P19(inset): Jim Parkin/Fotolia; P20-21: Jeff Greenberg/Alamy; P21(inset): Mario Burger;
P22(inset): Richard Seaman; P22-23: Richard Seaman; P24-25: Joshua Sherurcij; P25(inset): Q2AMedia image Bank; P26: Ian Marlow/
PhotographerDirects; P27tl: Q2AMedia Image Bank; P27cr: Jim Parkin/Fotolia; P27bl: Mario Burger; P28-29: Shutterstock; P30-31:
Shutterstock.

Art Director: Sumit Charles
Client Service Manager: Santosh Vasudevan
Project Manager: Shekhar Kapur
Editor: Penny Dowdy
Designer: Ritu Chopra
Photo Researcher: Shreya Sharma

Printed in Malaysia
1 3 5 6 4 2

Contents

What Is a Fire Engine?

A fire engine is a machine that fights fires. Some fire engines put out fires. Others rescue people.

These fire engines hold and spray water. Some fire engines can pull down walls. Others can carry people. Have you heard the sirens? The siren means someone needs help.

Some fire engines are not trucks like these. They might be planes or boats!

Pumper Truck

A **pumper truck** carries a pump, a hose, and a **tank** of water. The truck pumps water out of the tank, through the hose, and onto the fire.

Cab

Connector

The pumper truck's hose connects to a **hydrant**. The hydrant gives the firefighters water. This way, the truck's tank does not run out of water.

The truck's hose hooks up to a hydrant.

Boom

Hose

Firefighters ride in the cab of the truck.

Ladder Truck

A ladder truck has a ladder to reach fires. The ladder can also reach people trapped in buildings. The ladders are much taller than the ones you have at home.

Emergency light

Ladder

The ladder truck has extra emergency lights so drivers see the truck coming.

Hook-and-ladder trucks have hooks for tearing down walls. Trucks must be very powerful to pull down the walls of a building!

Firefighters use the ladder to spray water on the top of a fire.

Hose

Tool box

E2

VICTORIA
FIRE DEPARTMENT

WINFIELD PUBLIC LIBRARY

Tiller Truck

The ladder on a **tiller truck** is taller than the ladder on a ladder truck. It is carried on a **trailer**. The trailer attaches to the truck.

Rear cab

Aerial ladder

Bucket

Ground ladder

Tool box

Hatchet

TRUCK 15

Tiller trucks carry more people and equipment than a regular fire truck.

Tiller trucks are as long as two trucks!

Tiller trucks can be very long. The tiller truck needs a driver in the front *and* back of the truck!

Tanker Truck

A **tanker truck** holds more water than a pumper truck. Tanker trucks help when there is little or no water near the fire.

Cab

Engine

A tanker truck has a pool for water. Another fire truck uses the water in the pool. The tanker gets more water from a lake, swimming pool, or a nearby hydrant.

The canvas pool holds water so the tanker can go get more.

Tank

The tanker carries water to a fire.

Quint Truck

Quint means "five." A **quint truck** has five tools. They are a pump, a tank, a hose, a high ladder, and a ground ladder.

Siren

You can see the ground ladder on this quint. The high ladder is on the other side. The tank is inside the truck.

Fire departments can buy one quint truck. It is like having three trucks in one!

This is an old-fashioned quint truck.

Ladder

Pump controls

Rescue Truck

A **rescue truck** carries special tools. The truck helps in fires and other emergencies. It is smaller than a hook-and-ladder truck. Small trucks can be a big help.

Cab

Rescue trucks have tools like the **jaws of life**. This tool can bend metal, like a crashed car. Rescue trucks also have bright lights to help firefighters work in the dark.

The rescue truck has tools like the jaws of life inside the tool chest.

Tool box

The rescue truck may be small, but it's a big help in emergencies!

Brush Truck

Fires burning away from roads need a **brush truck**. When fires break out in woods or fields, brush trucks can get close to them.

Searchlight

Hose

This brush truck
fights a grass fire.

Tool
box

Brush trucks are
smaller than tankers
and pumpers. Brush
trucks do not get
stuck in the mud,
and they can park in
the woods.

Brush trucks have hoses and tanks
like the bigger fire engines.

Mobile Command Post

A **mobile command post** gives firefighters a place to make plans.

Cab

Mobi

Com

OEM1

The mobile command post has phones for communicating.

This truck does not have tools to fight fires. Instead, it has computers and phones. It is very important for workers to keep in touch with one another.

Satellite dish

Office

...mergency ...nd Center

City of Miami
Police Department
...e of Emergency Management & Homeland Security

The mobile command post has an office inside where firefighters can work.

Airtanker

Some fires are difficult to reach on the ground. An **airtanker** fights fires from the air. It holds water in a tank inside a plane. The plane flies over the fire and drops the water.

Helicopters are airtankers, too. They carry buckets of water to dump on fires.

Wing

Engines

Airtankers have to be very strong to carry heavy loads of water. They are sometimes called *waterbombers*.

Cockpit

Tank

Airtankers fight wildfires and other fires that trucks cannot reach.

23

Fireboat

Sometimes a fire breaks out on a boat or at a place near the water. **A fireboat** can come to the rescue.

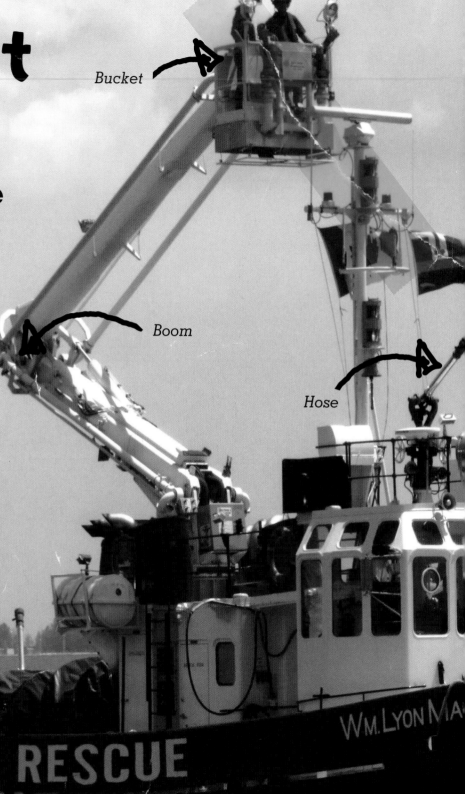

Bucket

Boom

Hose

WM. LYON MA

FIRE RESCUE

Fireboats work in an amazing way. They take water from the sea and pump it out from the bottom of the boat. Fireboats always have a supply of water at hand.

Look at all of the hoses this fireboat has!

Fireboats never have to refill their tanks!

Summing Up

Firefighters use a lot of tools to fight fires. They need many machines to carry and use these tools. Trucks carry ladders, hoses, hooks, and water. Special tools like the jaws of life help workers rescue people.

Quint Truck

Pumper Truck

Brush Truck

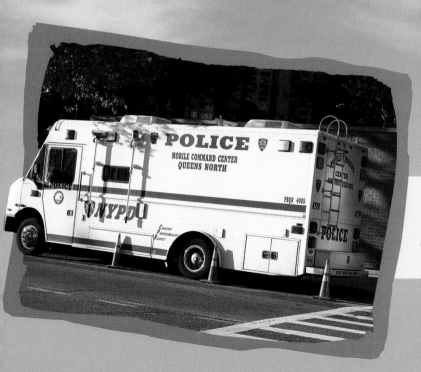

Mobile Command Post

Amazing Facts

- Horses pulled tanks and ladders many years ago.

- Dalmatians kept the horses company. These dogs became the good luck symbol of fire departments.

- Fire hydrants are different colors. This shows how fast the water comes out of them.

- Firefighters wear different colored hats to show what job they have.

- People should not park in front of fire hydrants. Hoses cannot bend or curve around cars to reach hydrants.

- Fire Prevention Week always includes October 9. This is the day the Great Chicago Fire of 1871 started.

- A new quint truck can cost over $400,000!

Glossary

airtanker an airplane that fights fires

brush truck a truck that fights fires in fields and forests

fireboat a boat that fights fires

hook-and-ladder truck a truck that contains a ladder and a large hook

hydrant a pipe in the street that provides water for fighting fires

jaws of life an emergency tool that bends metal

ladder truck a truck that has a tall ladder for high rescues

mobile command post a truck that has an office, phones, and computers

pumper truck a truck that pumps, or brings up, water from a tank

quint truck a truck that combines five tools

rescue truck a truck that carries tools to help in emergencies

tank a container that holds water

tanker truck a truck that carries water to fires

tiller truck a truck with a taller ladder than a ladder truck

trailer the back part of a truck pulled by the front

waterbomber an airtanker

Index

Web Finder
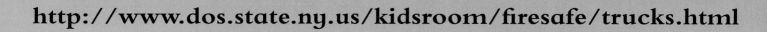

http://www.dos.state.ny.us/kidsroom/firesafe/trucks.html

http://www.nfpa.org/sparky/firetruck/index.htm

http://www.michiganfirehousemuseum.org/